Bodhisattva

How To Be Free

TEACHINGS TO GUIDE YOU HOME

NICOLE GRACE

Bodhisattva
How To Be Free
Teachings To Guide You Home
Published by Mani Press
369 Montezuma Avenue, Suite 415
Santa Fe, NM 87501

Book cover design by Lisa Delorme Meiler
Painting of "Peaceful Vajrapani" by Janet Piesold/Visuddhimati
Book layout by Rachelle Painchaud-Nash

ISBN: 978-0-9747852-3-3

Library of Congress Control Number: 2009940919

MANI PRESS
SANTA FE

For My Students

Foreword

I feel honored to be asked to write a foreword to this beautiful book. I met Nicole Grace during her visit to Bhutan in 2009 and it was the beginning of a beautiful association.

This book, *Bodhisattva: How To Be Free – Teachings To Guide You Home* is a breath of freshness. It sings loudly the profound messages of the Buddha in the practice of compassion and tolerance.

The words are appealing and so simple to comprehend. Anyone who wants to get a sense of Buddhism should read this book. This book also reminds me of a saying, "easy reading is damn hard writing." In particular, Nicole has managed to bring about the essence of Buddhism and the art of Bodhisattva practice in an effortless and simple manner. I want to congratulate Nicole on her accomplishments as a teacher and a writer.

I trust that readers will enjoy this book as much as I did.

Tashi Delek!

Her Royal Highness
Ashi Kesang Wangmo Wangchuck
Bhutan

Table of Contents

Introduction

What is a Bodhisattva?

The word is Sanskrit and translates literally as "enlightenment" (*bodhi*) and "being" or "existence" (*sattva*). Buddhists believe that a bodhisattva is a particular kind of enlightened being – one whose compassion runs so deep that he or she resists a final dissolution of the soul into Eternity until all sentient beings have themselves attained liberation from suffering. The bodhisattva will continue to reincarnate in unenlightened worlds, at great personal risk and at times with considerable agony, in order to serve as a beacon of light, guiding seekers to higher consciousness and, hopefully, Ultimate Freedom.

There are two kinds of bodhisattvas: the "ordinary" and the "noble." These terms indicate beings who have embraced the bodhisattva Way, but have not yet attained their own enlightenment: "ordinary"; and those who have attained a true enlightenment: "noble." These words may have unintended nuances in the English language – most would agree that both types of bodhisattvas are unconditionally "noble."

Bodhisattvas embody what is called *bodhicitta*. *Bodhicitta* refers to the penetrating intent to attain enlightenment for the sake of all sentient beings, while also bringing all seekers to Union with the Infinite. In *The Great Path of Awakening*, Jamgon Kongtrul instructs initiates to begin every meditation with the following prayer, "with intense respect and devotion... a hundred or a thousand times":

> "I pray for your blessing, my guru, great and completely worthy spiritual friend. I pray that you will cause love, compassion and bodhicitta to arise in my mind." [1]

---

[1] Jamgon Kongtrul, *The Great Path of Awakening*, trans. Ken McLeod. (Boston: Shambhala Publications, Inc., 1987), p. 8.

The *guru* can be an incarnate Teacher, or a disincarnate being that one has taken to be one's Teacher. Or, we can interpret the word *guru* by its literal translation from the Sanskrit, meaning "dispeller of darkness." So, anyone or anything that dissipates the ignorance (darkness) in your consciousness is your *guru*. Before attaining full enlightenment, bodhisattvas pray daily to that which will dispel the darkness for the desire to relieve others' spiritual pain, as well as the capacity to actually do that, until that quality – *bodhicitta* – permeates our awareness to the core and forms our primary motivation for any thought or action.

Unlike *arhats*, enlightened souls who do not seek out suffering beings, bodhisattvas can and will enter hell itself to rescue willing seekers and drag them out by the hair if necessary *without getting trapped in the burning flames themselves*. Bodhisattvas are truly the firemen or special forces of the inner worlds. Like firemen with their fireproof uniforms, shiny red trucks equipped with reserves of water and medical equipment, bodhisattvas must have extensive tools at their disposal and go through rigorous training in order to survive their descents into the scorching depths of seekers' confused minds and still emerge with their own freedom uncontaminated. Like the elite U.S. Army Special Forces with their motto of De Oppresso Liber ("To Liberate the Oppressed"), bodhisattvas have cross-trained in multiple skill sets, and then are dispatched by the Dharma to remote and perilous corners of the world to penetrate enemy forces and free those who cannot disentangle themselves. And, like all of the U.S. military special operations forces, such beings voluntarily submit themselves to these assignments at extraordinary risk to their health and even their lives.

Practicing as a bodhisattva requires living in the world without becoming seduced by it, nor overly repulsed by it. It requires dealing with the world and all of its tragedies, temptations and complexities, while remaining inwardly immune to its influences. We cannot escape to a monastery, convent or cave and shut everything out but Light, prayer and the company of others equally intoxicated by God. No, modern bodhisattvas need to have furniture and pay taxes, sit in traffic and shop for groceries – and yet must still remain serene and compassionate, one-pointedly fixated on enlightened consciousness, regardless of any disturbance, enticement, challenge, or the day-to-day deafening wails from the misery of unenlightened human life.

When some of us think about the extraordinary compassion, generosity and bravery of these beings, it becomes an all-consuming pursuit to dedicate ourselves to the advanced practices necessary to one day become a heroic spiritual servant as they have.

In the *Bhagavad Gita*, Krishna explains to his disciple Arjuna:

> "Who burns with the bliss
> And suffers the sorrow
> Of every creature
> Within his own heart,
> Making his own
> Each bliss and each sorrow:
> Him I hold highest
> Of all the yogis."[2]

The path of the bodhisattva is treacherous and at times strains even the purest beings to the limit. Yes, but those who have followed this path faithfully, devotedly, know that it also brings the greatest rewards.

When you come to understand that no one is truly separate from another – that we are all just waves arising from one vast ocean of consciousness – then you realize that there is no pain that is not your own pain, and no ecstasy that is not also your own ecstasy. In the appreciation of non-duality – the understanding that there is only the one Ocean, and that Ocean is Infinite Love – we naturally accept into ourselves both pain and bliss and everything in between. This may seem shocking, but in fact, this practice transports the practitioner to ecstasies hard to imagine or describe, like a small rowboat delivered hundreds of feet into the air by a tsunami. Through the bodhisattva path we can rise to heights far beyond our individual means in a more conservative practice, all the while increasing the size of our boat. One day, as the Indian saint Ramakrishna described, we can become "like big steamships, which not only cross the ocean themselves but carry many passengers to the other shore."[3]

The great bodhisattva, Padmasambhava[4], also known as Guru Rinpoche[5], said:

---

[2] *The Song of God: Bhagavad Gita*, trans. Swami Prabhavananda and Christopher Isherwood (New York: Mentor, 1954), p. 67.

[3] M, *The Gospel of Sri Ramakrishna*, trans. Swami Nikhilananda (New York: Ramakrishna-Vivekananda Center, 1992), p. 500.

[4] *Padma* translates as "lotus", and *sambhava* translates as "born from." Together, the name means "born from a lotus flower." The name refers to Padmasambhava's miraculous birth as a fully formed child of eight from a lotus flower floating on the surface of a lake. King Indrabhuti discovered the child. He observed that wherever the child was set down, a lotus spontaneously appeared, and noted, "'This child is truly a lotus-born one!'" Yeshe Tsogyal, *The Lotus Born: The Life Story of Padmasambhava*, trans. Erik Hein Schmidt (Boston: Shambhala, 1993), p. 7.

[5] Guru Rinpoche is commonly translated as "Precious Master."

"For anyone, man or woman, who has faith in me, I, the Lotus Born, have never departed – I sleep on their threshold."

Indeed He does. Bodhisattvas are always "on duty," watching our backs, offering assistance. Could anything be more comforting than knowing that? And could anything be more compelling than the promise of one day returning the favor, by becoming oneself a servant of the Dharma, qualified to stand guard? Well, not for a bodhisattva.

Composing the verses in this book became a vital part of my own practice of *bodhicitta*. I pray that by reading them perhaps at least one person may feel a sense of rapprochement with his or her own struggles and realizations and, with that, the will and joy to persevere in this most unusual occupation.

May everyone who seeks Light, find it.

May everyone who finds it, have the desire and capacity to share it with as many others as possible.

May we all be so fortunate as to experience the fulfillment of all of our sincerest prayers.

Finally, if there are any words in this book that create confusion, or which betray errors of understanding, the fault is entirely my own and in spite of the most prodigious efforts of my Teachers to raise me to their own impeccable heights.

Beach Stroll

The cool March mist hovers and wafts
A drunken cauldron of salt and clams
Sun crystals the sea in scattered shafts
My toes carve columns in the wet sand
And lofting on the morning drafts
Rides in silent peace one lone grey pelican.

Alone as he I breathe the air
Of time and life rolling out in bursts of foam
Fortune and failing, acts unkind and fair
As inevitable as the tolling of a metronome
This buzzing world is a country fair
We browse, buy and eat – and then we go home.

A tumble of craggy rocks up ahead
Signals the end of this day's stroll
And in the moist grains where I nearly tread
Someone has drawn a large heart still whole
Despite the tide, declaring inside: Susie + Fred
We may boast how unconquerable is our soul
But the sea's endless pace portends all flesh's deathbed.

I bow to the reminder life has given me today,
I see bobbing along in the dark blue waves a buoy
Oh all moments – even mundane – are part of our spiritual pathway
That bright orange speck in the sea is me… no, just a decoy
Buddha said all things that arise must one day pass away
So I treasure transience, as my walks go on forever, in joy.

The pelican and I exchange a knowing glance
He beats his wings against the current and flies
Into the wide sky, as we swoon in this heating trance

Sunlight burning off the fog as the lighthouse horn cries
Its last, the vast blue clear now, as water washes away all romance
My feet lift, and wings flapping, waves crashing, into Eternity,
   we rise.

Blossoming

Fierce winds marked the
Awakening Spring
Blowing into some future time
That chill lodged for months
In sparse branches.
My dogwood held strong
Green berries bumpling from its
Charcoal arms
I wrapped myself around the trunk
Pressing my cool cheek into
Creviced wood
Imagining a beating heart coaxing
Thick sap through its bare limbs.
Back soon,
I whispered
To my quiet companion
Keeping company with me through
That long winter.
I drove away with my tree
Reducing to a grey bud
In the rearview mirror.
Four days later my
Rain splattered windshield could
Barely contain the
Vision
An explosion of white
Flowers
Carolling from those branches.
They say transformation is a
Process,
That blossoming
Takes time
But now I know

The laborious flow of change
Happens deep in our veins as we only
Appear
To hibernate in silent stasis, and then the
Final flowering
Comes in a breathless
Surge
The seeds poised and waiting
Bursting forth in what only seems to be
One moment.
My dogwood splayed across the grounds
Was at once singing an exuberant
Vernal chorus and
Sighing
In profound relief
To be shining at last
Its most glorious.

Hope vs Faith

Faith is rooted in
Belief
Hope is rooted in
Doubt.
When you hope
You are also
Believing
Your desires may
Not come to pass,
Which is why you must
Hope…
When you have
Faith
You are
Believing
Everything will
Work out
For the best,
Which is why you can be
At peace…
Faith is
Positive
Hope is
Negative.
Faith makes you
Happy
Hope makes you
Anxious.
Enlightenment is
Love.
The opposite of love is
Not hate, but
Fear.

Enlightened minds have
Faith
Unenlightened minds
Hope.
Love without fearing
Live without doubting
Faith is
Peace.

Flock of Thoughts

Take time
To gaze into the sky
With no purpose
Other than to just be
And be quiet.
Be a witness to your thoughts
Watch them as though from afar
Like a flock of migrating birds
Specks of grey,
Then flapping wings,
V formation, then
Gone.
The flapping in your mind
No more yours
Than the birds are
Passing across the
Blue expanse.

Begging Bowl

I can see
The aspens
Soaking the Sangre de Cristos
In gold.
After the last rain
The air turned cold
And when I watch the
Sunset now
My cheeks and ears prickle
Pink.
Just a few days ago it seems
Pinecones dangled
Bright green
And sticky with sap
From the festival of trees
Here in the wilderness.
With a bowl in my hands
I go around them begging
Like an old monk
For a few pine nuts
Tucked like babies in a crib
Into the crooks of the cones
Dark and tanned now
And spread open
Yawning mouths showing their little teeth.
I have to pry and shake the cones
And then the tiny nuts
Drop like coins into my bowl.
Sap still coats the cones
And covers my fingers in sticky film.
The cones and the nuts
Cling to my skin,
No more drops in the bowl.
Yellow needles fallen

Drape to my black dress
Like filings to a magnet
Turning me into some
Strangely formed tree sprouting
Flesh and sap and sun-worn needles.
I'm done here
Nature has offered me
All she can
Since every inch of me now will
Trap any offering before it can enter my bowl.
I know there must be a way
A better way
To collect these nuts
To work around the sap and somehow
Not have it end up on me
Like a blanket of glue
Wedding me to everything I pass or touch.
The sap clings to me for days.
No amount of soap or oil or remover
Can get it off fully and I just give up trying.
I wait.
Two weeks later,
On a morning stroll
The skies streaked with the dyes of
Crushed roses
Mist hovering between the
Pine painted hills
Crunching ground under my feet
Reveals
Pine nuts
Hundreds, thousands of them
Perfectly dark and dry
Uncoated and supine
Resting gently in a carpet of shed needles.

Kneeling down
I lean over and start plucking them.
There is no sap
No stick
My fingers come clean.
I pull out the bottom of my dress
Dropping in seed after seed.
When my hands and ears grow
Red and numb
And puffs of fog leave my mouth
Like little balls of rice
I fold my dress hem up to my waist
Holding close my
Precious gifts
Standing up slowly
Not to lose a single nut
And return home.
This world can be consumed
But carefully
And only
In right time.

Soaking In

After weeks of drought
The rain comes
But the drops only
Roll across the cracked earth
Pine needles decorated with
Millions of watery pearls.
It is after days of
Soaking in these downpours
That the land can drink in
The bounty,
That the bejeweled trees can
Accept nature's offering.
While the dewy greens are
Very pretty, and the
Running streams make the most
Gentle trickling sounds
There is no healing until the
Water is absorbed.
It is like this with Teaching.
It is not the students who can
Reflect back to us the prettiest effect,
In fact they are the driest soil and
Needing the most time to benefit…
But it is the seekers, after years perhaps
Of being plied with heaven's outpouring,
Whose moist ground
Can at last
Absorb Truth.

Murder of Crows

I stepped outside
To feel the temperature
And took a breath
Of pure ice
Making my eyes
Water
Protective tears.
The cawing of the crows
Called out
Across the valley
Deafening shrieks
Echoing off
White mountain peaks
Stabbed with pines
Glaring sun shone the
Black black wings
Into metal
Hundreds of birds
Massing in a furrow
Circling
Rising
Screeching in a
Dizzying cacophony.
I wiped my eyes dry
And went back into
The warmth
Cheeks burning
From the change in climate
Outside to inside.
I closed and locked that heavy door
And stood for a
Long moment
In the quiet
All the more appreciated

After the biting cold and the raving ravens'
Assault
On my senses…
Thoughts can
Confuse and unsettle
The mind
But there is a
Haven
We can return to
In meditation
And though the
Thoughts might continue
Their mad circling and crying
We can always enter a place
Where we can no longer hear them
Or see them
Endlessly beating their midnight wings.
Let them fly and scream
While we sit in the warmth
In the pristine silence
Inside.

Bodhisattva

One night
I woke up in the dark
After rough dreaming
Only to see
Padmasambhava
Reaching his hand
Down to me
To lift me up
Out of that miserable state
And I realized
In that instant
That in his truly
Infinite compassion
He wasn't helping me
Because I had earned it
In some way – that I
Deserved his help.
It wasn't because of
Who I was
But rather
Because of who
He is.
Bodhisattvas just
Help.
They help because
They can and
Because that is simply
What they do.
That revelation has helped me
Through
Countless other nights
And days,
The relief and peace of
Knowing

These beings are around
Reaching down a hand
Whenever we need them
Not because of our greatness
But because of Theirs.

Spring

It was a long
Winter.
I watched the leaves
Drop off my newly planted
Apple tree
Leaving bony branches
That shook
In the wind.
Then came the snow
And I imagined
How cold
Those spindly arms must be
Right down to the
Skinny trunk and
Roots.
I saw the wet April
Blizzards
Wrap themselves around
My tree
Like icy hands.
Pity, I thought,
I suppose I will have to
Plant another one this year...
A few weeks later
In the glow of the Spring sun
I noticed my tree was
Covered
In new sprouts
Like a field full of tiny green gophers
Peeking their heads out of
The branches.
Could it be?
I would not have believed
My tree would survive

That winter,
Entering those dark days
So new and fragile.
I gaped at the buds
In wonder
And in shame.
I had given up on my tree
But I should not have.
I must not make that mistake
Again.

Be Here Now

Be here
Now.
The past and the future
Are but dreams.
We spend so much
Time and energy
Wringing our hands over
Events in the past,
Or glorifying them;
And either swooning over
Potential outcomes in the future,
Or desperately worrying about them.
If you can transcend
Ordinary consciousness
For a single moment
You see that there is, actually,
No time at all.
There is only NOW,
The eternal present,
The infinite breath.
The future is created by mind
The past is remembered by mind
But beyond mind is perfection
And bliss everlasting.
The only way to live constantly with
Joy and serenity and power
Is to keep the mind resting
In the present, the *now*.
It's like balancing on both feet
Keeps us standing straight and strong,
But if we lean forwards or lean backwards,
We lose balance and can fall
Or get knocked over.
So be here now.

Keep your mind focused on
What is happening around you
Right now:
The sounds, sights, smells, tastes, feelings.
If the present moment is painful
Resist the urge to dream about the future –
That is an artificial escape that keeps you
Tethered to the worldly plane.
Rather, go into the pain
Like swimming into a waterfall.
You'll get soaked
And then you'll be through
To the other side.
On the other side of pain
Is enlightenment.
Be brave, be strong
Stop dreaming new stories
That keep you bound in this dream world.
Instead
LIVE.
Breathe here and now
Be here and now.
The illusion will shatter
And you will be left standing
Strong and joyful
In the magnificence of
Truth.

Malicious Code

The Dark Forces
Can change your mind
Like a software virus
That reconfigures your computer
Right under your fingers.
What did you do to bring on
This attack?
Did you open a file that had been
Tampered with,
A document or application
With malicious code?
Now they're inside your world
Oh violation!
You can't trust your own thoughts
They've been
Viciously altered
Taking your familiar data
And twisting it
So you see only the
Reality they have modified in you.
What's true?
Hard to know...
Do your loved ones
Really love you?
Wouldn't it be better
To go off alone
Leave everyone so you don't
Contaminate them,
Or remove yourself from
Circumstances you no longer
Trust?
That's what they want
Coax the little sheep
Away from the flock

Then you're easier
To take.
What's the game –
The point of the virus?
Very simple
The hackers are not
Philosophers
Just thugs:
Quit.
Stop
Seeking Light
Sharing Light
Feeling Love.
They don't want any more of that
Beauty
Unleashed in this world.
Quit the Path
And the pain will stop.
Keep fighting for Light
And we'll make you
Forget
Who you are
We'll make you believe
You will never
Be happy again.
Well
You can take your
Deal
And shove it
Up your hard drive.
If quitters end up
Sad and washed up
Second string criminals like you
You're not exactly

Seducing me.
If I have to feel pain
To have the privilege
Of sharing Light
I'll take that deal
Any day.
I'd rather have
Sunshine
Coming out of my
Processor
Than smoke.

Faith

Faith
Is not
Believing
The invisible hand
Of God
Will catch you
If you fall
Taking a step
Into the Unknown,
Rather
Faith is
Not caring
Whether you are
Caught or not,
Being willing
To fall,
Seeing falling
As a fine
Outcome
If that is
What is
Right.

Passing Storms

I stand under the roof and watch the
Rain fall
In crystalline columns
Mile long chandeliers
Draping down from a
Puffy charcoal ceiling.
The columns move slowly
Across the valley
Painting prisms on the
Glinting green mountain walls.
And I see our moods and thoughts
Passing across the landscape of
The mind
If we sit quietly
In the cavern of Eternity.
In meditation we mustn't become
Involved in each raindrop
Wondering where it will stray next,
Fearing its imminent demise in the
Soaked desert soil, or
Clinging to the story of where
The storm began or
Who it touched before...
But be witnesses,
Warm under the gentle canopy
Of a still mind
Watching the storms
Trail their strings of jewels
Until they move on,
The clouds part,
And they fade in the brilliance
Of the emerging sun.

Just Love

How do you meditate?
There are so many
Instructions and
Rules:
Close your eyes,
Sit up straight,
Clear your mind,
Still your thoughts,
Gaze the Light behind your eyes,
Focus on a chakra,
Listen to the music!
What a project!
Instead of turning this
Sacred act into
An intellectual chore,
Try this:
Just *love*.
Meditation is love.
It's being *in love* with
Eternity.
Follow all the rules –
They help.
But don't make this
Intimacy
So complicated
When it is so very
Simple.
Just love.
And when you feel
The Universe
Loving you back,
You will be meditating
And you will never want
To stop.

Practicing

A student began saying,
"The other day, when I was meditating…"
At which point I interjected,
You mean, when you were
Practicing meditation.
Meditating and
Practicing meditation
Are two very different things.
Practicing meditation is something
You do.
Meditation is something that
Happens *to you,* usually after a lot of
Practice…

Peace

Peace is
Total contentment.
Without longing
For anyone or
Anything,
No hoping
No wondering
No worrying
No remembering.
Experiencing each moment
In its utter fullness
Hearing the wings of birds
Beating through the air
Breathing in the sweet, sage-perfumed
Morning after a rainstorm
Watching cloud tendrils flush fuschia
In the setting sun, and
Stars rise shining from the darkening sky
All without even the thinnest veil
Of thoughts, of the
Wax of past or future musings
Coating your sensing.
Peace is life
In richest color
In orchestral surround-sound
In pounding-heart exhilaration
Free
Alive
Alone
In your mind
Yet expanded to the edges
Of infinity.

The Risen

Unfurled uniform
Folded flag
Shiny buttons and
Multicolored ribbons
Battalion of stone shoulders
Rising from shores of fresh grass
Leaves may dry up and
Fall
In their red and gold autumn
But heroes,
No.
Their season is
Eternal spring
Blossoming, ripening
Rising
Rising from the earth
Tall stalks of wheat
Fruit of all of our
Greatest good
Golden harvest of humanity's crop
Preach to this choir
Singing the glory of
The brave and strong
Yea though I walk through the valley
Of the shadow of death
I shall fear no evil
For thou
Warrior
Were with me.
Now you are risen
And I am blessed.
This storehouse is full
Of holy grain.
Amen
Amen
Amen.

Rings

Rings within
Rings
Within rings
The Wheel of Dharma
Turns and turns.
Every attachment,
Desire
Aversion
Need
Binds us to
Another ring.
Some rings can help us
Survive perilous waters
Orange saviors
Tossed to us from sailing ships
That we can cling to with love
And Faith.
Other rings can bind us
To dark, magnetic forces –
Lethal necklaces
They seem innocuous
At first
Perhaps even
Breathtakingly attractive
Then they crush us
Like a serpent
Coiling around our necks
That at first
Seemed like a
Simple rope
A lifeline to safety.
In fact, the holiest rings
Can be the most deadly…
They may be the ones that bind us the tightest

And which are the most difficult
To pry our desperate fingers from.
We must keep our
Eyes clear
Wipe away the grit that gathers
From life traumas
Obscuring the true Way.
Touch the rings carefully
All of them.
Use the rings of Light to
Guide you and protect you
But be careful
Be vigilant
And remember:
The Wheel of Dharma
Is the ultimate Ring
From which
One day
We must all
Let go
To be
Free.

Tapestry

You meditated
With your Teacher
In a place of power
Soaking in the dyes of
Ecstasy
And thus
The fabric of your soul
Has been re-threaded
With filaments of light
Into a new design
Luminous tapestry
Draped over Time
Waving in the
Winds
Of your lives.

Overdose

When you have
Overdosed on the
Drug of Maya
And become
Unresponsive or
Comatose
Your spiritual teacher
May be forced
To extreme action
To save you
Before you can go into
Cardiac arrest,
The death throes
Of the heart...
At this point
If you are very lucky
This doctor
Of the soul
Will shove
A syringe of Truth
Into your heart,
Adrenaline of Light,
So you
Wake.
It may be painful –
Even horrifying –
But it works.

The Journey Out

I first see the wasp
In my peripheral vision,
A thumb-sized, hairy thing
Floating towards the windows
Facing the valley.
I turn my head to watch its
Journey,
Strategizing how best to get it
Back outside.
Unlike a proper bee, which
Flies with such purpose,
Buzzing in a straight, quick
Sprint from one place to another
Compact and efficient
The wasp dangles in the air
In no hurry at all
Creepy in its
Silent meandering
Its long spindly hairs for legs and
Probing antennae
Like the ears and nose
Of the elderly
Oddly elongated by
The weights of gravity and
Time.
The creature is certainly lost.
I assume it wants out
Into the fresh air
So in a heroic gesture
I throw open the front door
Wide
And prop it there with a
Silver pail
Stuffed with kindling.

I stand by the door and watch.
The air is cool and smells of
Fresh pine
And cedar firewood
And morning.
Wild lavender
Leans left in the breeze
And the scent floats through
The open door as well
Surely proposing an
Intoxicating invitation
To my wasp
Now dangling at the corner of another window.
It floats down and then
Of course!
Towards the door
Hovering for a moment in the
Mix of inside and outside air
Then mystifyingly
Turns and flies back into the house
Taking a new but not now unfamiliar
Tour around the room.
It flies to each window,
Rubbing its antennae against
Each pane
Then up to the ceiling.
I stand at the door
Incredulous.
Wouldn't any wasp
Want to be free
If given the option?
What is it doing
Back in this closed space?
Is it possible it feels safer

In a prison that it knows
When faced with the option
Of a freedom it has forgotten?
I think of its practice of
Throwing itself repeatedly against
Hard glass
And consider it has
Scrambled its brains this way
Too confused to tell the difference
Between freedom and bondage now
And allow myself a mean chuckle
At its expense
Before returning to my role
As hero and liberator
Of the poor thing.
I wonder if wasps can
Read thoughts
If they're sensitive to psychic projections
And try to press my mind into
Its miniscule brain:
You want to fly outside
I encourage it
The door is open
Freedom is good and happy
And awaits you
Now fly out out
Be free!
I repeat this mental nudging
Until I am convinced beyond doubt
That it has no effect whatsoever
On the creature's motivation
As it is clearly determined to
Fly everywhere in the room
Except by the door.

The scents outside flow in again
On the breeze
And I marvel that this tiny beast
Isn't moved by the beauty
It could know in
Just seconds.
And I remain
Standing by the door
Far enough away from the threshold not to
Frighten or deter
The wasp's path
But close enough to observe
The moment
Should it occur
When the wasp will fly out.
I feel myself a supportive
But somewhat imploring
Force
There by the door
Waiting and watching
This most indirect journey.
The wasp finishes another tour
Of my obviously fascinating ceiling
And then floats slowly down
Towards
Yes?
Yes!
The door.
It hovers a moment
Considering the options
And then decisively,
Quite at speed,
Tears off
Into the great beyond.

I move the pail away with a foot
And close the door.
One small, hairy
Manifestation of Light
Has found its Way.
All in all
It's a very good day.
I have done my job
And with that floating
Insect out of the house,
Two of God's creatures
Can now be happy.

Hades

We fill ourselves with
Food and sleep,
Sex and compliments,
Pomegranate seeds
Eaten by the handful
Red juice dripping
To our chins.
Bound thus to the
Darkness
We only dream
Of Spring
Of sun warmth and life
Growing in multicolored rays
Shining up from the earth.
If we could only learn to
Fill ourselves
With Light
And eternal, penetrating Love
We would never be
Hungry
Again.

Change

How many people
Declare their dedication
To the Pathway to Freedom!
They sit quietly
Projecting sincerity and earnestness
Blinking their eyes at you
Bowing with reverence and
Lifting their chins listening to you
Speak ancient words of guidance and
Tell stories about historic saints and prophets.
I want enlightenment! I want freedom!
You hear them thinking loudly.
Ah but do you want
What you must do
In order to have enlightenment, freedom?
You ask them, silently, of course.
And sadly, you know the answer.
How many people will successfully do
What one must do
In order to traverse the Pathway?
As Krishna says in the Bhagavad Gita,
"Perhaps one only..."
Will you be that One?
You could.
Anyone could.
All you have to do is change.
You have to become someone who
Is free.
If you, who you are today,
With your desires and requirements,
Self-importance and insecurities,
Could be liberated
Then you would already be liberated
And you wouldn't have to play this game

Of projecting piousness,
You wouldn't be so
Frustrated.
So obviously,
Something has to change
In you.
Enlightenment
As the lucky few discover
Is not really an attainment.
It is not a getting of anything,
An acquisition.
It is not a new presence of
Peace and serenity and wisdom.
Enlightenment is an
Absence
Of ego.
It is a letting go of
Everything.
It is a surrender,
Not a grabbing.
It is not more of,
It is less.
You can't get through the
Doorway to Nirvana
With your ego intact
Any more than you can
Shove a grand piano
Through a mouse hole
Try as you might.
Jesus said,
"It is easier for a camel
To pass through the eye of a needle,
Than for a rich man
To enter into the kingdom of God."

Rich, not in material wealth,
But in the Zen sense of being
Full.
Having an overflowing cup
Of Ego
Into which
Eternity cannot pour
Even a single drop
Of Her ecstatic knowledge.
If you are so
Rich with importance,
Identity and self-righteousness
Or embarrassment and self-loathing
Then you cannot possibly
Enter the Kingdom of God.
Why?
Because the Kingdom of God
Cannot enter *you.*
How can you empty the cup?
How can you empty your giant bank account
Of ego?
Change.
Will you be
The One
Who will give up your
Riches
For Freedom?
Would you give up even your life for it?
Only you can decide
Only you can empty your pockets.
It may seem insurmountably difficult
To even conceive of
Letting go
Of who you are today,

Well
I suppose if becoming
Truly liberated
Let alone enlightened
Were easy
Everyone would be free
And this world would be a
Very different place
Now wouldn't it?
Change won't happen to you
Just because you're patient
And a nice person
Meditating every day and
Thinking good thoughts
So stop waiting around for that
Like a hungry person
Who sits obediently
In front of the oven
Projecting goodness
And wondering why
No food is getting cooked.
If you want to change
Then change!
Stop whining
Stop waiting for a more
Convenient day
Some future, better time
And just do it.
This world needs more light.
So just stop complaining
And get out of the way
So light can shine through you
As it was meant to.
Turn your teacup over

And spill everything out
To make room for
God.
Then
You will not be filled with "you"
Anymore
But with perfection.
That is the right kind of change.
That is Freedom.

Teacher Moon

Round goddess
Emerges
From a mountain
Sea
Dripping silvery light
Smiling at us
Knowing her power
And reveling in Its
Display.
And in her
Incomprehensible
Brightness
I see
Our potential,
How we can strive to
Reflect Light
Blinding if viewed directly
But through this
Intermediary
We can witness
Monthly
As much magnificence as is possible
With our earthly eyes.
It is the moon's
Compassion
That allows Her to lift Herself
Before our to date unworthy gaze
Unrobed,
Resplendent,
Showing us at once
Her Glory, and also,
What we could someday
Become.
We must hear Her,

Understand Her
Showmanship
As a challenge and a
Calling and,
If we resist,
A shaming.
Be Her student,
Turn yourself from
The shadows
A little bit at a time
And then one day
Rise like that
Yourself.

In a Dream

In a dream
Friends, lovers, apparitions
Morph and shift
Come and go
Objects rearrange
Nature appears in
Odd hues,
Talking to us,
Food
Sings and
We dance and fly
And sometimes
Run.
In a dream
We feel
Slightly confused
Our minds foggy and
Complacent
As bizarre events unfold.
Our heart breaks
Or we are frightened
Silly
Or we make love to
Strangers.
We start tasks that never complete
And entwine ourselves in stories that never resolve.
Welcome to Life
In the world.
The only constant
Force,
Our only true
Refuge
Is in Light.
Oh bring the glory

Shine that joy
Forever
In our minds
Stop the babbling, the
Incessant
Commentary and
Dullness
Fruitless frustrations.
Wake into
God,
Lush
Palace of ecstasy
And Safety,
Operatic pulchritude,
Womb of truth.
Stop chasing
Phantoms,
Floating endlessly through this
Maze of lies.
Wake
Wake
And
Be
Free.

Humility

In the news today:
A 13-foot long Burmese python
Exploded
Trying to eat a 6-foot long
Alligator
In Everglades National Park.
Rangers were unable to locate
The python's head...
Proof that there is
No Teacher
Greater than
Life.

Discrimination

On a long drive
Through winding mountain roads
Teetering on the edge of
High cliffs
I saw an
Explosion of trees,
Pines,
Oak,
Cyprus,
Evergreen trees,
Trees in full
Glorious bloom
Ringing loudly with
Magenta and purple
White and yellow.
There were bushes
And flowering plants,
Rare medicinal herbs,
All arrayed and available
To see and taste and use
In varying and ingenious ways
The locals understood after
Centuries
Living an unspoiled life
By the land.
But use any tree, any herb
Incorrectly
And beware!
There are countless
Poisons and curses
To be found here
For the uninitiated
Or the merely careless…
How to tell

Which flower
Which herb
Will heal or harm?
Ah, that is the question.
How to tell
Which tree
Which bush
Requires which offering
To which deity?
Another important question.
Discrimination is
All that stands between
Health and destruction
Enlightenment
And suffering.
Let the world teach us
In time
To know the difference
And before then
To humbly practice
Extreme caution.

Covered

It snowed last night
Light dusting of powder
Covering the ground
The trees and all of mountain life
Gently touched
Like a cool hand on your shoulder
Comforting you
Saying,
I am here.
In a few hours
The snow will melt
And all will be as it was.
I long for a great storm
And then another
And another
Until one day
The snow will cover us all
And will be too thick
Too encompassing
To ever melt away.
Every pine needle and
Shiny stone and
Insect wing
Covered with snowflake crystals
Glistening under the sun
Indistinguishable
One from the other
And we will see then
That there is nothing but snow
That we are all made of this
White glory, and
There will never be
Anything else.

The Project

You turn every step
Of the Pathway to Enlightenment
Into a project
Something to achieve
To conquer
Or to procrastinate over...
You try to turn
Love Itself
Into an object to obtain,
Grabbing at it,
Missing the whole point.
You have managed to take
Oneness
(Simple enough – there is only ONE)
And twist it into
Twos and Threes and Fours.
It's always about YOU and
Then God I suppose
And everyone else,
The ones on your side
And the ones who are fighting you.
So much work
So much paranoia
So much self-importance.
Now take a deep breath and
Listen:
What if you are seeing this
All wrong?
Maybe
It's just not that complicated.
Maybe there is
Just LOVE –
Love that is in every particle of existence
That IS every particle of existence.

You are made of that love
And if you are
Very quiet
And still
If you stop stirring up the water
Obscuring it with all that swirling sand
You will finally
SEE
And understand.
Oh...
You will say,
I,
The center of my own universe,
Don't even really exist
Not in the way I thought.
Oh God...
There is only
Love.

Eclipse

The moon
Reflects
The light of
The sun.
Our great star
Burns up its very core
To give us
Life.
You could fit 1.3 million Earths
Inside the sun.
The moon is about one fourth
The size of the Earth.
The outer layer of the sun is
11,000 degrees Fahrenheit.
The moon averages between -387 Fahrenheit at night,
   to 253 during the day.
The moon is 2,160 miles in diameter;
The sun measures 864,000 miles.
And yet...
On a regular basis,
We observe the
Moon perfectly align itself
Between us and the sun
Blocking that massive flaming sphere from our sight.
We call it a
Solar Eclipse.
The moon superimposes itself upon the sun,
Day turns to night.
Amazing
That something
So relatively small
Can totally obscure our view of
Something so much greater
So much brighter.

As Hermes Trismegistus said,
As above
So below.
We must always practice
Careful discrimination
When considering the
Source
Of Light
And
Life.
For things are not always
As they appear...

Treasures in Time

We grieve
Absence.
When something
We love or
Have come to rely on, or
That we have built
Our identity upon
Goes away,
We dress our
Consciousness
In black,
Sit in dark rooms,
Weep.
But every emptiness
Creates an opportunity
For that space to be filled
By something – or someone –
New.
We glorify the familiar
And want what has left us
We cower from the precipice
And resist the
Tingling terror
Of the abyss.
But if we could only
See
Out into that chasm
See
Into the shadows
Of the future
We would be instantly
Too excited
To mourn,
Too breathless with anticipation

To even remember our sadness.
Every loss is immediately replaced.
Nature does not indulge
Any vacuum.
If we can embrace
The promise of great treasures
Lying in wait
In the shadows of Time
If we can perhaps even
See
Golden threads of sunlight
Illuminate faint prisms of the
Jewels heaped before us
We can
Step forward
Bravely
Into tomorrow's promise.
In every absence
A presence arises.
Focus on what you will
Gain
Not on what you have lost,
Dress your mind in
Bright color
Sit in the light.
With so much
Beauty
Yet to be experienced, and
With your hands open
To grasp the great gifts
Of the future
You will have no way
To clutch futilely at the past.

Frost

At first
It looked like
A field of smoke
Rising from the earth
Until I realized
It was a frozen lake
Releasing a layer of
Evening frost
To the rising sun
And I saw our
Hardness
What becomes of us
During those cold
Nights of the soul and
Then
How the morning comes
Burning through the coating
Over our hearts
Sending up smoke and fog
Before the air clears
In the warmth
And the drama subsides
As we are melted
Back into
Clear
Still
Water.

Be Mine

Eternity called.
She wanted to know
If you would be
Her Valentine.
She promised she would
Always
Be with you,
Love you
Forever
Unconditionally,
Show you
Unlimited
Unimaginable ecstasy, and
If you could just
Love Her
More than you love
Anyone or anything else
She will make sure that you
Never feel
Lonely,
Anxious,
Fearful,
Angry, or
Lost
Ever again.
What should I tell Her
If she calls back?

The Best

People
Listen carefully:
Even if you
Took everything
I own,
Moved into my house,
Wore all my clothes and
Captured the attention of anyone
I have loved
You would still
Never be me
So stop
Wasting your time.
Better to cultivate
Your own Self
Your own Way.
Then instead of
Becoming a
Shadow of someone else,
An amateur imitation,
You can be the
World's only example
Of the best of
Yourself.

Enlightenment First

A student travelled far
To visit a levitating Yogi,
Amazed by such mastery
Over gravity.
The Yogi described years
Of intensive daily practice to
Finally
Raise his body above the ground.
The student asked him,
When do you meditate?
The yogi answered,
I don't have time.
The student noticed that
Sitting in his chair
He was at equal height
With the levitating yogi.
He left immediately and
Spent the rest of his life
Practicing meditation
Intensively,
Finally attaining freedom.
Don't confuse
Siddha powers
With Enlightenment.
You can be an
Impressive magician
And yet remain
Selfish, jealous
Arrogant and mean,
But you can't have
Any of those weaknesses
And be
Enlightened.
Once you are

Truly Free
You can have
All the powers in the universe
And you won't think they are
More important than Light
Or, that you are.
Always remember:
Enlightenment first,
Then siddha powers.
If you seek powers first,
Enlightenment may
Never come.
If you seek
Enlightenment first,
Then whether powers
Come or not,
You will not care,
Nor will any
Sincere student of yours.
Seek the dissolution
Of Self
Not the displays of Self
And you will
Transcend
Not powers alone
But all desire to have them.

Box of Evils

Hope was the last
Evil
To escape
Pandora's Box
After all the darkness
Had been freed
Into the world,
After anger, jealousy,
Hatred, lust, and pain.
What everyone misses
Is how
Dangerous
Hope can be, too.
Give that up
Quickly
If you want freedom
Or you will be trapped
Waiting
For expected outcomes
To disappoint you,
Shatter your dreams
And make you weep with
Longing for what you will see
You cannot have.
Hope is the opposite
Of Faith.
Faith is expecting
Nothing
Knowing you will be given
All that you need
To be free
Generously and
Without your prayers.

Hope arises –
And we cling to it –
When we stop
Believing
We are safe and
Perfectly cared for
By the Eternal Protector.
Faith was never
In that box of evils
Because it didn't belong.
Faith has the
Power
To fight them
All
And prevail.

Koala Zen

Oh adorable!
Sweet and furry
Zen master of the Outback
Chewing his leaves
Perched in the nook of a Eucalyptus tree
Contemplating the essence of life.
But screw with him
Serene and
Cute as he looks
And those sharp, black claws
Will tear your face off.
Lesson learned.

Wild Ride

We have ideas about our journey
Through this world -
How it should look
Who we should be traveling with -
Our minds like a dead man's hands
Clawed in cold rigor
Around unbending views.
We want
And our wanting
Is a sickness.
We sweat and bend
Nauseated
Over the limp corpse
Of freedom,
The freedom of not having
Calcified ideas
Of how our work or love or circumstances
Should be now or how they will
Unfold.
You don't want to be
So miserable,
Feel so trapped and
Unrequited.
But what to do?
Imagine you're at Disneyland visiting
Mr. Toad's Wild Ride
Where you're clutching the steering wheel
And jamming your foot on the pedals
Of a car that is
Completely controlled
By remote electronics
And not
By you.
If jerking the wheel around

And stamping on the pedals
Gives you an important sense of participation
Then knock yourself out.
But there is another way.
You can simply be satisfied having
Made the choices
To visit Disneyland
To walk over to this ride
To step into the car
And then
To realize that you have now
Willingly given up control,
That you have accepted the fact that
The brilliant engineers and designers
At Disneyland
Have designed this ride to be fun
And safe
And, yes,
A little bit *wild*.
You can just step into the car
And enjoy the experience
Instead of trying to manipulate
Where the car will go and
How fast
When there is no point.
Then you can just let go,
Put your hands up in the air
And feel the wind on your face,
Listen to the laughter and screams
Of the other participants
And just watch
How it all plays out.
Thousands, perhaps millions,
 Of people have gone on this ride.

They have all walked away
None the worse for the experience.
Some ride it again right away
Others try out the other rides in the park
But no one, yet,
Has ever made that wheel
Do what they wanted it to do
So why waste energy trying?
Stop.
Uncurl your fingers from the
Wheel of your life.
Trust Eternity to guide you
Once you have decided
Where you want to be
And what type of ride you want to visit:
Worldly or spiritual.
Get the major structures in place
And then
Let go.
See where this ride takes you.
Be unafraid
Trust the Great Engineer
To show you
An unbelievably
Magical time.

The Freedom of Alone-ness

True freedom
Is the ability to feel
Absolute contentment
And peace
When you are utterly alone.
When you do not have a
Sweetheart
A lover
A best friend
To open your heart and
Make you feel warm and admired and needed,
To reflect back to you
What you hope to believe about yourself,
But when you must believe in yourself
Anyway.
When you can wake up in the morning
Knowing that no one is going to call you
"Just to hear your voice,"
No one is sitting at home thinking
About the wonderful possibility of spending time with you,
And yet,
You are completely at peace
With your own life
Your own day
Your own thoughts,
Then you will be free.

Pure Love

So few really know how to love.
Most people love with attachment.
They love with *need*.
As long as they are getting something back, they can love.
Otherwise the love becomes contaminated
With sadness
Resentment
Frustration
Anger.
Real love has no requirements.
You just love.
The only way to love purely is to let go
Of any need to have anything in return for your love.
Open your clenched fist
Clutching desperately
To an idea of yourself as the object of the other person's affection,
To a self-worth based on being someone who is loved,
To being a person who is loved by someone so wonderful.
Love and need, love and need.
There's an undercurrent of bitterness there
Laced through the sweetness of open hearts
Sharing yourselves with each other
Celebrating moments of joy
But always with the lurking shadow of
What if
Always with the gnawing rat inside the walls of
What the person should have said, but did not,
Should have done, but did not,
Said and did, that you wish they had not...
Who is this person now?
After the ripeness of passion fades into familiarity
The shadow grows longer
The little rat chews and chews all night long
And you are sad and frustrated and

There's that awful sense of
Loss.
You love now, you feel that you still love, don't you? Don't you?
But where did this person go that was so perfect?
Why can't they be like they were?
Think now –
Is the object of your focus the only one who changed?
Were you ever really in love? Did the love just fade?
No. No, this isn't how it works.
You were in love, but not purely.
What did you love then?
You loved this beautiful person,
Who appeared to you bathed in the glow of your own projected
emotions.
Your emotions are familiar to you.
You know your own light.
Everyone loves himself enough
To love the one that reflects himself back, favorably.
You loved this other person,
With the need for them to behave a certain way towards you
To not be needy of you in ways you weren't prepared to provide
for them.
So the love was tethered to earthly hooks
And could not rise
And when the earth turned on her axis
As she does
The tethers pulled and tore
And the love was shaken and moved.
Pure love has no tethers
No requirements
No needs.
When the earth moves, the love moves with her.
In fact
Pure love transcends us all.

Human love comes from the mind and emotions.
Divine love comes from the Infinite mind within us.
You love
You just love.
Whether you are given something in return
Or not.
Whether you are loved back
Or not.
How can you love like this?
You love like this because "you" don't love per se
You allow the Eternal within you to love
The Eternal within others.
Then it is just God loving God
Which is perfect
And pure
And unbound
Always.

Saving Lives

I asked a pre-med student once:
How many lives do doctors save every year?
He shook his head gravely,
Overwhelmed by having to conceive of such a great number.
"I don't know exactly," he said, "but a lot."
No, I said to him,
The number is zero.
Only God saves lives.
Doctors simply prolong them.
A great many of us do good work
Here on earth
Contributing as best we can
To humanity
According to our interests and our skills.
But let us keep it all in perspective, shall we?

Time

Jesus said, *This, too, shall pass.*
Buddha said, *All things arise and pass away.*
We hear these words of wisdom and think,
Let me not get too attached to this love,
This beauty,
This comfort,
This joy,
These welcome circumstances
Because I might lose them.
Quite true.
But what we forget is that,
In our moments of
Fear, pain, loss and loneliness
That the darkness
Will pass, too.
That the suffering which has arisen
Will also pass away.
What seems an inconceivably positive outcome now,
May never arrive
And yet, the circumstances you will find yourself in
In time
May very likely surpass
Any you might have considered earlier.
Your mind was simply not evolved enough
Creative enough
In your pain
To believe that such beauty
And wonder
Could come to you.
What will bring this joy to you
When you can least believe in it?
Time.
We cannot rush resolution, much as we would will it.
We can only wait, patiently,

Faithfully.
You may not believe in God
But everyone believes in Time.
Jesus said, *Because thou has seen me, thou has believed.*
Blessed are they that have not seen, and yet have believed.
It is easy to have faith today.
And much more blessed to believe in what we cannot see:
The gifts of tomorrow.
Giving in to despair
Is like running away from home
Christmas Eve
When all your gifts so lovingly wrapped
Await you under the tree
Never to be opened, discovered and enjoyed.
Life wraps our many gifts
But only Time can open them.
Time is the Great Healer.
In time,
All wounds of the heart will mend.
Be patient.
Time will heal you. It will.

Aspens in Fall

My hair lifts
In a crisp
Gust
As the round
Golden leaves
Shimmer
Caught in the morning
Light
Thousands of coins
Rustling
In the sky
Another sharp wind
And they
Fall
Raining
Heavenly treasure.
We are
All
Rich
Beyond
Imagining.

Empowerments

Empowerments are gifts from Eternity
We can plug ourselves into the Earth itself
And recharge
Like a cell phone
Going from low battery to
Charge Complete.
This re-energizing has to be used
Just right.
But often the opportunity is wasted.
We all want to be happy and carefree, but
We must seek lasting happiness and enduring freedom,
Rather than the transient varieties.
Most people get their batteries charged
And use the power to feel good for a while
Coasting on the energy.
Oh the laughter
The high feeling
The light in our eyes!
Then, inevitably, the power runs out.
The battery goes back to zero
And the joy is gone.
You're lethargic and sad;
Work is dull;
You don't remember how you could have
Felt so happy
Such a short time ago...
No, this is not the Way.
As soon as you have the good fortune
To receive a precious empowerment,
To sit for a few hours in a Power Place on earth,
To have an extraordinary meditation,
To be with your beloved Teacher
In form, or just in your heart;
Put the Light to work!

Dedicate yourself with new vigor to your dharma task,
Apply yourself with greater intensity at work,
Exercise your body to exhaustion if you can,
Meditate with particular focus and intent,
Use every last atom of power in this way
And you will find something extraordinary:
Your empowerment will generate a
Constant stream of Light through you.
By using the extra energy to improve yourself,
You will heighten your awareness level.
By heightening your awareness level,
You will have higher meditations,
By having higher meditations,
You will,
Little by little,
Become free.
Empowerments can change you temporarily,
Dropping you back down to your original mind states
Once you have expended all the energy feeling good.
Or,
Empowerments can change you permanently,
Raising you up to new, transcendent mind states.
The choice is yours.
Freedom takes work.
Freedom requires postponing
Immediate gratification
For enduring satisfaction.
Use power wisely
And power will make you wise.

Illusion

On a warm summer afternoon
Light clouds drifting through the
Blue, expansive, desert sky
I sit quietly and watch Nature
Buzzing and chirping
Pine needles stirring
Tiny lizards skittering across sun-baked stone.
An electric green blur of little wings
Whirrs past my nose
Then launches straight up into the air
Higher and higher, till it
Plunges straight down below the tree line.
It darts back up and over to a long, flowering stalk
Poking a needle beak into the tufts of gold at the peak
Utterly still there, but for the wings,
And then he's off again, disappearing into the heat.
A light breeze lifts a few loose hairs from my face
Christmas lights sway above my head
Long since unplugged
Forest green plastic dangling clear droplets.
Lavender stalks cup their palms and
Softly blow their fragrance at me
Purple kisses.
The hummingbird returns
Little fury
And hovers
Wings beating madly
Above my head
Touching its bitty beak
To the hanging lights.
It flits to one teardrop of glass
Then another
And another.
Strange flower

Scentless and not at all
Sweet.
There is no nectar there for you!
How could this creature be so confused?
The hummingbird tries
And tries
To extract some kind of
Juice
From this swinging tangle
Of manufactured beauty
Holiday decoration
Not even performing its temporary function.
How can this little being
Tiniest heart beating under neon feathered breast
Not know the difference between
This braided-wire mirage
And the throbbing, textured, fragrant magnificence
Of a real flower, alive?
But here it remains,
Buzzing from one glass droplet to another
Ever hopeful
Of extracting nectar
From this empty, mute artifice.
How like him we are.
Ever expending our energy
Hovering hopelessly
In front of one plastic joy after another
Mistaking the barren illusion for
The effulgence of Truth
And never tasting
The radiant ambrosia
Never hearing
The operatic chorus
Of Perfection

Though it is all around us
Practically screaming
With everlasting Life.

Sacrament

Breathe deep
The morning sun
Filling your every cell
With the radiant oxygen of sunshine
Exhale the poison
Of worldly pursuits.
Nourish your Temple with
Rays of life force from a golden setting moon
And purge the holy chambers
Of confusion and ignorance.
Take into yourself the
Scented magnificence of trees and wildflowers
And release cravings and doubt.
Breathing itself can be
An act of prayer
Or a gorging on illusion.
So drink from the
Currents of enlightenment
Not the streams of desire
And you will become the ocean itself.
See the world as an infinite garden of Light
Your body as God's palace
And every act
Becomes an offering
To the Divine,
Your whole life
A sacred poem
To Love.

Sailing

A deep fog has
Settled in the hills
Low and thick and
Misting the world into
Silence
I hold onto the
White wooden railing
Framing the terrace where
Trees and brush and mountains have been
Wiped from the landscape
Vanished inside this enveloping cloud and
It is like I am
On the deck of a
Great ship
Sailing into the
Deep Beyond
Where even the
Prow has
Disappeared in the
Brume.
The sky darkens and
I feel that
Thrill
Which is very nearly
Terror
And my breath stops.
We could be floating towards the
Edge
Of a giant precipice
And would not know until the
Drop
But we could also be
Slipping into the
Endless waters of

Bodhisattva

Eternity
Unprotected and blind.
A light wind
Brushes across my face
My arms rise out and
I know that
In this fear and fog and
Helplessness
I am
Free.

Resistance

Everyone will tell you
"Change is hard,"
Transformation is the greatest
Challenge
On your spiritual journey.
But it's not true.
Change is not hard.
Resistance to change is
Hard.
If you let go
Surrender into the
Fear
Willingly
Open your fists and
Release
All you are clutching
And simply be still as the
Winds of transformation
Blow through you
Then everything in you that is
Not free
Will be carried away with the
Leaves and dust and debris
Lifted into the air and
Gone
And all that will remain
Is
Peace.
See?
Transformation is
Easy
If you stop trying so hard to change
And

Like a strong breath clearing a
Palmful of ashes
Just let the
Wind
Free you.

Control

Would you
Sit in the sand
Watching the waves swell in
And pull out,
Thin curling rolls
Building to
Great stretches of water
Bending into blue-green wheels
Racing toward white foam explosions,
And critique them?
Would you
Instruct the ocean
How to curve her waves toward the shore
More evenly,
To pace her tides
More conveniently
For you?
Do you berate the
Sandy water
Rail at it
Angered and offended
When she turns you
Upside down and
Pins you helplessly underneath her
Pouring salty gulps of
Liquid into your lungs?
All you were trying to do
Was have a nice swim…
What was she thinking?
How *dare* she be
So un-accommodating.
No.
Of course you wouldn't.
It would be silly.

But even if you did
Scream at the sea
Hearing your shrill voice echo out to the sky
Pound the surface of the water
With your fists
Splashing salt into your eyes
You would accomplish
Nothing.
The waves would not cease their
Infinite rolling rolling
High and low
Smashing into foam
Mist rising
The tides out and in out and in
Under stars and moon and sun shining.
You cannot bend this
Ancient creature
To your will
Much as you would like to.
So stop trying,
Stop trying and save your energy
For appreciating her
Instead.
I know what you're thinking.
You're thinking that if you just
Shut down your heart,
If you can stop caring
About the ocean
Stop visiting her and
Swimming in her waters
Forget about her completely
That then you will end
Your ceaseless frustration.
Perhaps you will succeed

In removing your problems
Loving the ocean
But they will just arise
Somewhere else.
Will you start wailing
About the sun now?
The nerve of him to shine so
Brightly
So hot
All day without any mercy.
Ha!
You accomplished nothing
But a pathetic escape from
Majesty and beauty
Wisdom and transcendence.
The only Way is
Humility.
Love the forces in life
That you cannot control
For the very fact that they
Are beyond your power
Even to understand,
Let alone
Master.
Soften then.
Let go of your
Arrogant strutting and
Fretting and
Whining.
Embrace the inconsistency,
Caprice and
Terrifying magnificence
Of these eternal waves.
Mastery and peace will come

Not from will and force and aggression
But from
Surrender.
Let go now.
Bow and
Touch your head to the sand.
Ask to be
Shown
The Way.

Contract

They knock on the door
Whispering sweet promises
Free cookies!
My, aren't you handsome? And spiritually powerful!
Come with me
I can get you everything you want
So much faster.
Don't listen
It's a lie
Sign the contract
And your nails will curl and yellow
Your teeth will rot
And your eyes will blacken and hollow out
Then you will only find fleeting moments of joy
By consuming as nectar
The anguish of others
And you'll be knocking on doors
Trying to sell your bitter sugar
For one cool breeze of relief
From the flames licking eternally at your putrescent flesh.

How to Make a Pilgrimage

Travel
Light

Selfless Giving

Selfless giving is a pathway
To Freedom.
The problem people have is that
They give with expectations of reward.
This is not selfless.
Reward is a salve to the ego.
With ego, there is Self.
Selfless giving is giving without
Any expectation of or desire for
Appreciation from the recipient.
It is giving without
Notching up your efforts on the wall
Like little conquests.
If you give your energy,
Your time
Your wisdom
Your love
And feel that it is a burden
That it was work
To serve another
Then it is not selfless giving.
Selfless giving is transformational.
When you are completely focused on
Relieving the suffering
Of another being,
Surprise!
You have no time to think about yourself.
When you move your attention to another
You cannot be thinking about what you
Don't have that you want, what you
Have that you don't want,
What you are and are not, and the
Unfairness or unpleasantness of your life circumstances.
When you are serving another being

An amazing thing happens:
You begin to feel better about your own life and
About yourself.
So selfless giving does
Reward the giver, after all...
We just cannot hope for this reward
Or any other
At the time we are
Offering ourselves to Eternity
As agents of Her work.
In order to attain enlightenment
You must learn to give selflessly,
Truly without need or attachment,
And to give that way tirelessly
Constantly
Until all trace of ego and desire
Are blasted from your awareness
By the force of the light and power
That selfless giving will cause to
Stream through your being.
Give of yourself
In order to lose your Self.
It is the only way
To be Free.

Forage

When the snow stops
Falling
The birds and bunnies
Chipmunks and foxes
Come out of hiding
Hopping and scampering in their
Forage for food.
When the worldly onslaughts
Slow their assault on us
We come out of our confusion
And, newly unencumbered
Begin our search
For spiritual sustenance
Seeds of Light
Scattered about
By the Holy Ones.

Now

When you project your mind
Into the future
Dreaming about
Circumstances
You hope might occur
Or that you
Dread
You are living within
The confines
Of your own mind.
When you remember the
Past
Stirring up emotions of
Pleasant nostalgia
Or of desperate trauma
You are living within the
Prison
Of your own mind.
But when you simply
Abide
Still
In the present
You are in the
Free and
Infinite
Expanse
Of Eternal mind.
The future and the past
Belong to time
And time is a
Construct
Of limited consciousness.
In the fullness of
The infinite awareness

There is no time
There is only this moment
Now.
The only way to live
In Peace
The only way to know
Truth
The only way to be
Truly free
Is to keep your mind
Here
Now.
Stop dreaming
Stop reminiscing
Let your mind
Expand to
Complete awareness
Of all of life
In the Present;
Then you will
Live
Not in
Your mind
But in
God's.

Othello

You think you're thinking your own thought
But you're not.
99% of the thoughts in your mind are not your own.
There are six billion people on planet earth
Each one a mini radio transmitter
Of psychic noise.
And then there are the little Iagos
Whispering whispering in your ear
Until you believe them.
What will cause you to snap?
There are thoughts you discard as ridiculous
And then there are the ones that start to seem to make sense...
They manage to wedge a toe in the doorway of your mind
And then they can leverage it wide open
Spiders of darkness
Weaving webs of insidious doubt and suspicion
Not your own
Coloring your world in shadows and pain
You have to be so careful
Look through the peephole first
Don't pull open the door with the chain on,
That's all the space they need to sneak in
Scuttle into the corners and start spinning.
You have to stop being so sweet
Oh it's all God
Yes, but God has many forms
And some of them want darkness, not light
If you want to be free
You can't deny they exist
Any more than a city girl can deny
Spiders crawl around the house in the country.
You just want to meditate
And be left alone.

But they just want to consume your pain
For lunch.
Don't open the door.
And if they get in, well,
Nothing slams the sole of your shoe down on them harder
Than Love.

Choices

A scraggly sparrow
Sat on the edge of
My garden
Clutching with both talons
A spool of loose packing straw
Larger than one of its wings
Which must have fallen
From a giftbox I opened out there
Days ago...
The bird was darting its head down
Towards the flowerbeds and then
Up in the Pistache trees shadowing them
Up and down up and down
Like a nervous twitching.
But then I saw the thick worm
Shiny and trailing a path
Through the soil
Supple and damp from the
Morning dew, and
I understood.
Ah, choices...
We cannot gather stuffing
For our nests
And with the same claws
Catch hold of our food.
We can pad our world
Or feed our souls,
For our tiny fists can
Clasp either material or
Spiritual nourishment
But not both, and yet
Still manage to lift our wings
And fly
Into the heavens.

No Fear

Attachments are
Bondage.
If you can release
All attachments
You will be free.
But how?
Realize that
Attachment is
Nothing more than
Fear.

What do you fear?
Make a list.
When you can believe
(Because it's true)
That fear exists only
When your mind is
In a state of
Confusion
That there is ONLY
Enlightenment
And enlightenment is
Perfect
Always,
And finally
That if you are nobly
Walking the Pathway
You will always be
Given
Everything
You could possibly need
To succeed,
Then you will
Stop being afraid.

You will stop
Fearing
Circumstances
That have not yet happened,
Fearing
Consequences of
Circumstances that happened
In the past,
Fearing
For your self,
Your safety,
Your happiness.

What counters fear?
Faith.
Not hope -
Which is just another
Attachment
To a possible outcome -
But faith.

Wanting and hoping
Agitate the mind and
Stir up the emotions.
Understand this:
You are
Always safe
In ever-present Light
Always loved
In holy Light
Always provided for
In every way necessary
In glorious, giving Light.

Breathe deep
The perfection of the
Divine.
Be still
In fearlessness.
Be Free.

Arrival

The glow appears
Behind dark crimson coated
Mountains, and
Moments later,
A silver crown
Peeks out into the
Periwinkle sky.
You realize you have
Stopped breathing,
Gaping in silent wonder,
As the curving hills
Slowly release Her
Full form to
The heavens
And you can't help but blush
Witnessing this majestic
Arrival.
She rests briefly
In the bend of the Earth
Before ascending and
Hovering between
Forested mounds,
A glistening bindi
On the world's
Bare forehead.
One day she will
See
For us
All.

The Pathway to Freedom

There are two fundamental types of
Spiritual pathways:
One for those who seek a better life
Now
And one for those who seek freedom
Forever.
The first pathway will almost never lead to
Enlightenment
In a single lifetime.
What it can do is get you to the point where you
Choose the second type of pathway
When you have had enough of feeling good
And you are ready to transcend both good and bad altogether.
The first pathway will indeed make you happy
Now
If you follow it correctly, with devotion and care.
The second pathway will make you happy in a very different way.
If you truly seek freedom
You will see that in order to attain it,
Sacrifices must be made.
Making sacrifices may not feel very happy
While you are making them.
The good news is that once you let go of something
In order to free your hands to hold more strongly onto Light
You change
You become someone for whom whatever you gave up
Is no longer a sacrifice at all.
You become someone who is not interested in
Whatever you let go of.
This process of change makes you happy
Gradually.
One day you realize that you have nothing left
To sacrifice.
You are free.

Freedom is the ultimate happiness.
But be forewarned!
The pathway to freedom
Isn't always fun
Unless your idea of fun
Is going through the wrenching pain
Of detaching yourself
From cravings and needs in the world.
The pathway to freedom
Isn't always joyful
Unless your idea of joy
Is working selflessly, impeccably as you can
Until you drop from exhaustion
At the end of each day.
The pathway to freedom
Isn't easy, ever.
But it is worth it.
When you cross the threshold
Into Nirvana
When you fall
Like a bead of perspiration
Into the Great Ocean
Becoming indistinguishable from That
Then you will remember
All your suffering for Freedom
All your days and nights of
Pain and sacrifice
And you will know without any doubt
That it was all worth it.
You will know that if the path were
Twice as hard and
Three times as long
That you would do it all again
For the privilege of feeling

The enduring peace
This one-ness with all of life
That you know, and that you are,
Now.

Happiness

How can you make yourself
Happy
When you're not?
It's all a matter of perspective.
If you can move your mind
To see the grandeur of the
Great Plan
The way everything always works out
If you're honest with yourself
Because how can it not?
Then you can perhaps
Be patient
In the short term
When you feel like the structures of your life
Are one by one dropping away
Like little cats that one minute are cuddling
Next to you
But when you look back down you see
They have padded off somewhere, away from you.
How did it happen?
How could you not have noticed them
Leaving?
So they are gone
And there's a sense of loss
The seat empty now, and not warm
But the seat is empty
Which leaves room for what is next
A new warmth
Will it come?
Of course.
You know that.
When you're being honest with yourself
And rational
You know from watching

The snow melt into flowers
That something else will come
And be warm
And fill that place.
If you're lucky
It will be the fullness
Of your own heart.

Urgency

As you scale the mountain of
Spiritual evolution
In your quest for
Freedom
You must feel that a
Menacing fire
Rages
At your heels
And that your most
Precious
Loved one,
The object of your
All-consuming
Lust, the
Only true
Comfort
You may ever know
Has been waiting
For you
Serenely
At the top
But could give up Her vigil and
Vanish
At any moment.
Don't be
Impatient
With Eternity
If you have not yet
Dissolved
Into Her
Complete embrace;
But do be breathtakingly,
Uncompromisingly
Impatient

With yourself.
Run now
Run child
Run to
Love.
Then you can
Rest
Forever
In the arms of God.

Dawn

Navy velvet sky
Sewn with diamonds
Hangs like a dark tapestry
Over the sleeping earth
Dark mounds lie silent
And still,
A beast in repose,
If you watch very closely
You can see it
Breathing.
In the East
Deep blue turns turquoise
And the thick skin
Grows purplish and then
Pink
Shadows form in the crooks
Muscles tensing and
Rippling...
The mind seems relatively
Quiet
Before the spiritual Path
Stirs its slumber
Illuminating
All the valleys and
Jagged cliffs,
Hard edges and
Adumbrations.
The colors of a
Waking world
Wash over the
Beast
Showing us its
Full form.
When the sun peaks overhead

The moving colors fade in the
Force of light
The shadows vanish
And the mounds
Grow silent.
The sky will turn
From blue to lavender
And then dark again,
But the beast is
At peace.
We will not hear him
Growl
Again.

States of Mind

Oh how happy I am! Life is great!
Everything is right in the world. I can help a lot of people because
of my joy.
Everything is miserable. I have never been so unhappy.
I was so much better off when I was happy.
I feel like I will never be happy again.
The illusion of high states of mind is that they are higher.
The illusion of dark states of mind is that they will go on forever.
Like geographical states
They are places we visit
For a time.
The trick is not to get trapped in them.
Wouldn't getting trapped in high states of mind be
A good thing?
Not if you seek freedom.
A locked cell is still a locked cell
Even if it is beautifully decorated.
The problem is that you can get stuck inside
Before you realize
The choice you have made.
So be careful
Be vigilant!
If what you seek is freedom...
Not a bird's eye view down at the problems of the world,
Not a hopeful view from down a deep hole, up at a circle of light.
But a constant gaze
Forward
And through
The veil between worlds.
Then one day
You will have the ability to feel at peace,
Content and happy,
No matter what state of mind
You are visiting

Today.
You will simply
Not notice
The difference.

Meteor Shower

The three nugget-sized
Rocks
Dropped
Out of the sky
Like charcoal hail and
Lay
Steaming
In the driveway.
I stood there
Motionless
Gaping at these
Glowing gifts
Bits of stars
Millions of light years
Old and
Far away.
Their suns long since
Exploded
In great bursts of
Power and heat and
Light
And yet
There at my feet
Were pieces of
That moment
That time
And I understood
That there is no time
No past
Because a star was shining
Here
Now
In my world, my home.
I gaze into the sky at night and

See billions of stars
That science tells us are
Gone, and yet
All of them are brilliantly
Alive in the celestial mirror
Breathing, in my own sights.
Our light
Our life
One meditation or
An entire incarnation of
Glory
Explodes out and travels
Forever
Landing some time
Some day
At the feet of
Whomever may be
Watching
Sparkling fire
In someone's heavens
For Eternity.

Undistracted

What is Enlightenment?
Perhaps it can be understood as
One's ability to remain
Unmoved by the distractions
Of the world.
If you can truly rest
Without thought,
Without inner disturbances
From the seductions
Of life,
Then you are
Free
From their influence.
When you simply don't
Crave
Anything
Apart from the experience of
Oneness
With Eternity
Then you are
Liberated
From the
Mind states
That cause anyone
Unenlightened
To attempt to
Satisfy desires
In the physical realm.
With all your heart
You may
Enjoy the pleasures of life.
But if you
Need anything besides
Spiritual love to

Make you happy
Then you are still
A pilgrim on the
Great journey,
Illumined perhaps
But not yet
Eternally
Free.
Enlightenment requires a
Special monogamy.
Eternity will only share with you
Her complete embrace
When you have decided
To share yourself with
No other lover
Greater in importance to you
Than God.

Spirituality

Spirituality is not
Religion.
Spirituality is a
Way of life.
There is no rule book for this life.
That is what makes it so hard
And so unpopular.
Spirituality is a perspective,
An aesthetic.
It is an expression
Of love.
Spirituality is not defined by
Outer manifestations of
Faith or
Holiness
It is not about what you
Eat or don't eat,
Wear or don't wear,
Read or don't read.
Spirituality is something that happens
In the quiet and privacy of
Your mind and
In the ever blossoming
Of your heart.
Spirituality is what you
Say and do and think
When no one else is there to see you
And admire your efforts.
Spirituality is
An intimate affair
Between you and Eternity
Breathing and living and loving
As One.

Language of Eternity

Silence is the
Language of Eternity –
Be Fluent.

Acknowledgments

I am grateful for both the intense pain and the great ecstasy that forced me to become a witness to nature and Life. Sometimes, when you have exhausted yourself from one or the other of those extremes, all you can do is watch, and learn.

I thank my Teachers, whose generosity and patience clearly have no limit.

And lastly, but not least in significance, I thank my students, for allowing me the privilege of sharing with them what little I have come to understand about Light, and life.

Nicole Grace is a Buddhist monk and author of the award-winning book, *Mastery At Work: 18 Keys For Achieving Success, Fulfillment And Joy In Any Profession* (Mani Press). She teaches personal and professional development seminars, as well as Buddhism, mysticism and meditation, to students around the world.

For more information about *Bodhisattva*, please visit us online: www.bodhisattvabook.com.